T0044867

Signs
in My Neighborhood

by Shelly Lyons

Consulting Editor: Gail Saunders-Smith, PhD

CAPSTONE PRESS
a capstone imprint

Pebble Books are published by Capstone Press,
1710 Roe Crest Drive, North Mankato, Minnesota 56003.
www.capstonepub.com

Library of Congress Cataloging-in-Publication Data
Lyons, Shelly.
Signs in my neighborhood / by Shelly Lyons.
p. cm. — (Pebble plus: my neighborhood)
Includes bibliographical references and index.
ISBN 978-1-62065-098-1 (library binding)
ISBN 978-1-62065-889-5 (paperback)
ISBN 978-1-4765-1727-8 (eBook PDF)
1. Signs and symbols—Juvenile literature. I. Title.
AZ108.L96 2013
302.2'223—dc23   2012023424

Editorial Credits
Sarah Bennett, designer; Svetlana Zhurkin, media researcher; Kathy McColley, production specialist

Photo Credits
Capstone Studio: Karon Dubke, 11, 13, 19; iStockphotos: Rebecca Grabill, 15; Shutterstock: A-R-T (background), 1 and throughout, Frontpage, cover, somatuscan, 5, Stacie Stauff Smith Photography, 21; Svetlana Zhurkin, 7, 9, 17

Note to Parents and Teachers

The My Neighborhood set supports social studies standards related to community. This book describes and illustrates signs in a neighborhood. The images support early readers in understanding the text. The repetition of words and phrases helps early readers learn new words. This book also introduces early readers to subject-specific vocabulary words, which are defined in the Glossary section. Early readers may need assistance to read some words and to use the Table of Contents, Glossary, Read More, Internet Sites, and Index sections of the book.

Table of Contents

What Is a Sign?

Signs tell us what to do.

They help keep us safe.

Look for signs

in your neighborhood.

Stop and Go

Eddie sees a traffic light.

Cars go on green.

At yellow, they slow down.

When the light is red,

cars stop.

What is that red octagon?

It's a stop sign.

Maya stops and looks

all directions before

pedaling forward.

A yield sign stands
at the street corner.
Sid's dad slows down.
He checks for cars
before crossing.

Safety Signs

When June walks to school,

she finds the crosswalk sign.

June crosses the street there.

What is that big H sign?

This sign tells people

that the hospital is

just down the road.

Pointing the Way

In Juan's neighborhood,

street signs stand

at each corner.

Juan's house is

on Village Square Drive.

Near her home,

Lisa spots a one-way sign.

It tells people they can go

only one direction.

Signs keep us safe.

They tell us where to go

and how to get there.

What signs do you see

in your neighborhood?

WATCH FOR CHILDREN

NO PARKING HERE TO CORNER

Glossary

crosswalk—a place where walkers can safely cross the street

direction—the way that someone or something is moving or pointing

neighborhood—a small area in a town or city where people live

octagon—a flat shape with eight straight sides

traffic light—a red, yellow, and green light that tells people and cars when to go and when to stop

Read More

Rissman, Rebecca. *What Is a Community?* Chicago: Heinemann Library, 2009.

Searcy, John. *Signs in Our World*. New York: DK Pub., 2006.

Van Lieshout, Maria. *Backseat A-B-See*. San Francisco: Chronicle Books, 2012.

Internet Sites

FactHound offers a safe, fun way to find Internet sites related to this book. All of the sites on FactHound have been researched by our staff.

Here's all you do:

Visit *www.facthound.com*

Type in this code: 9781620650981

Check out projects, games and lots more at
www.capstonekids.com

Index

Word Count: 164
Grade: 1
Early-Intervention Level: 16